Guys Have No Game

A Book Of First Impressions

Geoff Keith & Ian Gulbransen

This book is dedicated to whoever invented the Internet, so guys all over the world could show us their amazingly funny alter egos.

Contents

Introduction

Online dating used to be thought of as a last resort. I'm having no luck in the real world so I might as well head to the Internet. Well, those days are long gone. It seems like almost everyone is on some sort of online dating site whether it's for a niche group like Bikers looking to hook up, Christians looking to mingle and find someone to marry, or just the typical all-in dating site where you're hoping to find your true match who you can live with in perfect harmony. See what we did there? With the internet comes extra confidence when approaching a member of the opposite sex. How often do you see a guy walk up to a woman in a grocery store and say, "Yo, what up? Your titties are niiiiice! Hit me up sometime." Unless your grocery store is way more exciting than mine you've never seen that happen. But in the online dating world that is only a mild pick up line.

The idea for this book came about when our female friends would forward us messages they had received on whichever site they were a member of. Not only were they some of the funniest fucking things we had ever heard, they were real which makes it so much better. We asked a couple of our friends if we could use their pictures to set up our own dating profiles to see what funny messages we would get. Within minutes our inboxes were flooded. You post a picture with some boobs in a push up bra and every dude online wants to fuck you. It's science.

We were hoping to get a few funny messages here and there, but to our surprise about 20% of them were hilarious in one way or another. In a matter of weeks we had compiled thousands of funny messages from guys all over the country.

We never responded to any of the messages or egged them on in any way to get them to say what they said. Everything you read in this book is an online pick up line. Some are long, some short, and some make absolutely no sense except to make you crack up and thank God you didn't write something so stupid. We weeded through thousands of messages to use only the very best ones and we still have over 200 for you to enjoy which we broke up into different categories. We've blurred out their thumbnail pictures and their profile names and in the cases where they sent us a picture they really felt we should have, we put black bars over their eyes (this is the legal way of doing this...we checked with our lawyer who was laughing the whole time). Now all of these screenshots are funny enough by themselves, but there were some we just couldn't hold back on and had to add our own comments. You will see these after some of the screenshots.

We feel you men out there will enjoy this book because it gives you an insight into your competition, or lack there of, and you women will like it even more because you've probably been hit up by some of these clowns or definitely heard some similar stuff. So everyone enjoy and stay tuned for more books because we don't feel this online dating thing is going away anytime soon...

– Geoff & Ian

Lines That Never Got Anyone Laid

"If you were a booger, I'd pick you first."

– Anonymous Guy (Who Didn't Get Laid)

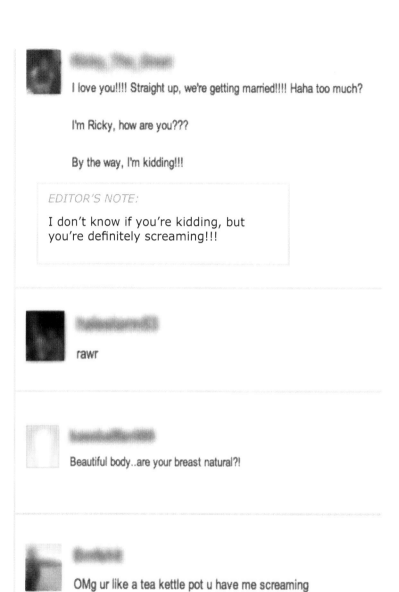

I love you!!!! Straight up, we're getting married!!!! Haha too much?

I'm Ricky, how are you???

By the way, I'm kidding!!!

EDITOR'S NOTE:

I don't know if you're kidding, but you're definitely screaming!!!

rawr

Beautiful body..are your breast natural?!

OMg ur like a tea kettle pot u have me screaming

Omg will you marry me ;-)........lol

EDITOR'S NOTE:
Nope

Your seriously my dream girl :) I mean based on those looks!! :)

Daaamn gurl you fancy

You look delicious! Let's flirt and who knows

what fckin cloud did you fall from hahaha!!!!!?:p

Well you seem a little too cool but like you said if we click we click

The following images were attached to this message.

EDITOR'S NOTE:

Nice trophy, he's letting us know he's a winner

You is fine girl. I need some of that

They yours... Both of em? ;)

Hi Hi. What kind of flirt skills ya got?;)

Love your boobs!

Hey girlll let's make some magic happen

EDITOR'S NOTE:

Abracadabra! Poof! You're gone

Hey put those away or let me have em;)

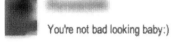 You're not bad looking baby:)

The following images were attached to this message.

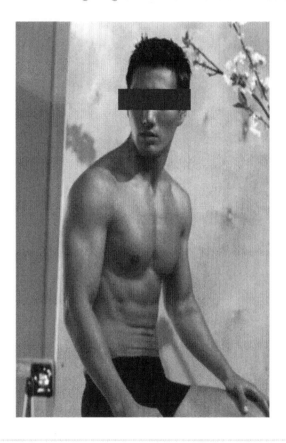

 Love your boobs!

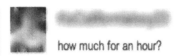

how much for an hour?

Let's fly to san francisco for dinner ??

How bout that weather lately ?

awkward smile :3

What's up ████████ that's an interesting first name. My names Alex.

What company do you model for ?

Hey whats up, Fuck me if I'm wrong but isn't your name helga? ;) lol that's my pick up line

Definitely not lame here. Will certainly rock your world :) I'd like to meet up with you some time and find out what youre all about - John

Im a good hearted man on the streets but a freak in the sheets, if you are interested in some good times hit me up.

Hello how rub doing ms) how r u doing on this awesome Tuesday? Ur really cute I'd like to get to know u better :)

EDITOR'S NOTE:
I am good, thanks for asking. I am good, thanks for asking.

If you were stranded on a deserted island and you could only take one thing with you, what would you take?

EDITOR'S NOTE:
My vibrator

Hi ████ I'm Mickey. How was your weekend? Do anything fun?

The following images were attached to this message.

Only difference between men and women is that a man can be bald and have a beer gut and still think he is sexy. Anyways whats up? And roscoe's is pretty amazing!!!

Wow you're an absolute knockout! I think "holy shit" is the technical term

Hi...I kind of feel silly sending this message - but what does DTF mean? Is that some sort of POF term?

(I just joined)

If you were an autobot you would be optimus fine. How's that for standing out haha

can I show you a good time! Im in vegas for the next two weeks and I would love to fly you out

> EDITOR'S NOTE:
> Baller!

Your so fine I wanna make you mine

Hey ███████ u look cool to converse with. I hope u respond so as can chat a bit! :)

EDITOR'S NOTE:
Broken English always turns me on

I seriously would hate to be your dad haha ;)

Not gonna lie.. Let's fuck, tonight. Say yes

how long do you want your next relationship to last?

Chuck Norris is the reason why Waldo is hiding...

haha my names kyle, hope to get to know you and possibly be friends and/or more.
Hope
to hear from you

EDITOR'S NOTE:

Friendship? I'm here to fuck

What up doe! Whats going on wit ya Baby girl? Nice pics!! Check me out and hit me back,
if you'd like.

My friends think I move too fast. Would you marry me? Oops!! I meant to just say Hi. :-P
Haha

Hey,I just met you,and this is crazy,but here's my number,so call me,maybe? Lol. I'm Luke how are you.

What should a first message say??
Hey what's up? Nah that's lame..
Hi sexy?? Creepy!!
Hi my name is DANIEL? Can be read from my profile..
I think you are beautiful?? Even though I do, seems to forward..
Anyway since I don't know what to write as a first message, I'm just gonna leave it at.. Hi
how are you? I hope we can talk sometime :)

> *EDITOR'S NOTE:*
> ## He realizes he wrote all that, right?

You look like a lil bit of trouble but a hole lot of fun ;)

> *EDITOR'S NOTE:*
> ## Oh, I get it. Hole. Nice. Like MY hole

Why couldn't the bicycle stand on it's own?

Because it was two tired!

Unique enough?

I would like to put a baby in you and a ring on you lol

I was blinded by your beauty so I'm going to need your name and number for insurance reasons

Let's go clubbing

> *EDITOR'S NOTE:*
> Note: this was the rapper Pit Bull

So, what's your favorite sport?

And that's the most absurd thing you've done in the last 6 months?

I know, kinda weak questions.. but you're gorgeous, and I'd like to talk to you and see if we click

Fun+Flirty=us msg me back if your interested

The Pitch

"I don't have a room full of writers pitching ideas.
It's just me, out of my head."

– Louis C.K.

hi ████ My name is Keith, i have alot of very interesting things that i have done and i have seen things that most will never see in their lifetime. I came on here trying to meet some new fun,interesting people.Grreesh "what a disappointment its been, I didn't expect to much thought. I live in Hbeach. I also am a photographer, i use to shoot hawaiian Tropic Pageants and venus swimwear models for years,.....What agreat time it was traveling all over the world and meeting alot of famous people.....I like the way you do your eye makeup, its just right, not over done......Ok for now, It would be great to talk sometime, this is a one time chance to meet a life long frined......Hope you well.....Keith :)

EDITOR'S NOTE:
"My name Borat! I like U. S. of A!

Howdy, my name is Tyler. I live in long beach and work on the queen mary. I go to school and im also in a improv group and film/ write sketches and shows constantly. My passion is acting. Im a busy person but I would like to find a lady to share my adventures with. figured id start the conversation so check out my profile and if you like what you see write back , can't wait to hear back..

P.s. yea your hot ill give you that but what makes you irresistible is you like the expendables! You did hear about #2 - jcvd and Norris! That movie is going to scare every terrorist in the world haha...well peace ..

P.p.s.s. awesome name I like it. Reminds me of someone you'll have to wait to meet me for that story.

EDITOR'S NOTE:
P.P.P.S.S.S. I'm gonna pass on that story

Hey [redacted] I was looking over your profile as I came across it and realized that there were a few things that I liked! I'm not too good at describing myself but I will tell you one thing about me, and that is I'm actually a great guy that has values, a genuine heart and will definitely treat you with respect (if it is neutral). I'm not here to play games. If you feel the same way, feel free to return a reply. I hope to hear from you soon! -Chris

> EDITOR'S NOTE:
>
> You want "neutral" respect? Not mutual?

I will change your life! After hangin out with me youll be bored with anyone else. I'll show you what life, spontaneity and adventure is really about. You will be pissed for wasting so much time on what you thought were real men. Not cocky, just confident.

Will this message stand out to you?? :)

U are super cool. Im gregory im 22 I'm kinda a stay home guy I like movies and tv shows and cars. But I also love To go out and have a couple beers with friends. I am a super faithful and honest guy. If there was an animal more loyal than I dog I would be that animal. I love to have fun and making people smile and laugh is one of my specialities! Along with massages haha. I am super funny and can always cheer u up :) Anyways I work full time in sales and i have a car. I like u. U seem very down to earth and you are super beautiful so reply back if ur interested.
Ps. I'm handsome and have a good smile haha :p

hey how are u im Niko:) im 21 have a career my own place a brand new whip(im proud)

ahha i am also a fashion marketing major at the art institute, i like yur profile u seem way kool and really honest i like tht and not to mention yur gorgeous:) i dnt know

y u on here tho lol well we shud def talk more:) oh and if u like men with tattoos im ya man haha

Hey I'm Justin. I'm from LA, but I'm stuck in Oceanside for the time being. I have a lot of tattoos, and all of them have a meaning of sorts. I love music of pretty much all kinds. I'm trying to think of something to make me stand out. Hmmm. I fight bees with my bare hands. It's a dangerous underground past time, but the pay out is good lol. Hit me up sometime!

Great nerd swag, I dig it. Here's about me. I'm funny as shit, listen to better music than most people, and am actually educated. I can articulate and spell, which apparently is a lost art. I'm sure you get plenty of messages, so if you don't get back to me no big deal. But trust me, I'm more interesting than the rest

> *EDITOR'S NOTE:*
> What's it like being better than everyone else? I have Bieber fever!

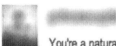

You're a natural beauty, simply Stunning...

I'm looking for friendship 1st...sound like a good starting point?

I'll keep you happy every minute!!

Well hello I promise you that meeting me will be one of the best thing you could and will ever do (:

Well hello there I don't say this to every girl but you very beautiful I'm such a down to earth guy that treats the girl I'm interested in like how they should be treated :) I would like to get to know you better and really see where it goes oh an I'm josh BTW thanks for your time reading this hope your day is going good :) hope to talk to you soon if your not interested could you let me know also just to be nice thanks

I'm sure you get a ton b/c you are beautiful....
But if you want a quality, athletic, classy, tall, good guy who likes to have fun.....let me knw
The "all around" deal is what makes me stand out! REAL and classy....

HI MY NAME IS CHAZ! And i really Want your attention! :) I'm a huge fan of the Notebook and a sucker for hazel eyes

So I know your ike a ten I'm like a 7-8 and I know your not superficial or anyhting but once you see my goods you'll know im a ten =) lol What do say? You want to shoot the shit together?

So would that be Colgate or Crest? Which ever it is your smile is a killer =)

Well getting to the point...my name is Paul. I live in Corona, have 2 little dogs (that think they're human), no kids(at least not that I know of), been a cop for 12 years....whatever else just as.

There's a lot to me that what I can write but it would be a lot of BS since you don't know me yet. I can honestly say I'll be one of the nicest guys you ever met.

Paul

well if this message doesnt get a reply then i guess you arent interested in a guy that can get down and dirty, flirty, fun, but all at the same time knows when to be serious and grown

Hey ‌‌ Summer is here, let's hit the pool and grab a beer! Hope my rhyme doesn't make me sound queer. Lol. Let me know if you're interested. I'm moving to a sick community with an amazing pool setup next week. I guess it goes off on weekends. Or we could just grab dinner or coffee if you'd prefer. Good luck gorgeous. Hope to hear from you.
David

you had me at "fun and flirty" ;)

So here's the email you've been waiting for (fingers crossed right) lol
I won't bore you with some cliche, cut and paste note, but I just created this profile and you're my first email so come check
me out, if you're interested...let's connect.

Here's another deal maker, I'm new to the area...so I promise you'll have my full attention (in a non clinger way of course) lol
Talk soon,
Jay (whispers....6'2 barefoot, athletic, goofy and rumored to be amazing lol)

I'm a real man, patient, understanding, and hilarious lol. (cuz it true) I would just like an oppprtunity of getting to know you. I'm starting to think women can't see a genuine man who for everything they looking for. Whatever you want in a guy I got it straight up. But you gotta get to know me before you conclude that. I can keep you smiling and shining. So if you interested let me know. I like the things you acknowledge, very in tune.

interested in a fun, mature, and a highly educated successful business man,? im arron so hows ur day gon?

hello hello
my name is joe
i am a fun guy to hang with
i am awesome about 95% of the time
the other 5% i am batman
and i would like to get to know you
message me back

your Spartan King is here my lady >:)

HEY SEXY I KNOW YOU DONT KNOW ME BUT I WANT TO GET TO KNOW U IF DAT OK WITH U WELL BOUT ME IS IM OUT GONIG FUN AND FUNNY TO BE WITH IM SINGLE LIKE YOU SEE I DONT PLAY NO GAME I KEEP IT REAL ALL DAY EVERY DAY IF U LIKE WHAT U SEE IF U DONT THEN KEEP IT MOVING IM PUERTO RICAN IM CALLIN FROM HIALEAH JUST MOVE DOWN HERE FROM OHIO BOUT WEEK AGO IM 25 YEAR OLD IM CLEAN SO WHAT IM LOOKING FOR IS A REAL ASS FEMALE DAT KNOW WHAT SHE WANT AND KNOW WHAT SHE NEED

EDITOR'S NOTE:

CAPS LOCK + BROKEN ENGLISH
+ DAT = KEEPER

Hi I'm Charlie I'm 18 I'm looking for a relationship. I'm very outgoing. I love to be outside. Most of the time I'm either hunting, out on the lake wakeboarding or inside at the gym. I love to go camping and go on hikes. I dress for success and try to look nice everywhere I go. I'm looking for any girl that wants to be treated right by a guy and loves to have a great time. I would be lucky to be with a girl as pretty as you. If you are worried that I am older, I can tell you that I'm not. I can send a picture over text or email if you would like

---

Hey boo I'm about to turn 21 in feb I know that's not much older but u are so stunning u have a perfect pettie body and a smile that makes me go crazy I'm currently in school for architecture so I need a new girl to take my mind off my ex. Ps I like to get naughty

Hello! A lady like yourself needs & should always have a good looking mature man like myself, in your life. Someone that smells good, fun to be with, humble, secure, %100 real, adventurous, loyal, fun & always cool, calm & laid back, in good shape. Dont cheat yourself, treat yourself & come get to no me.

Keith

Hey im chris im 23 i am italian i am a Mma fighter and i work in a retirement home i am huge on trust honesty loyalty and respect i love to cook i am a country boy at heart an d i love the outdoors if you like what you hear please get back to me i hope to hear from you soon

> **EDITOR'S NOTE:**
>
> Wait, you're a MMA fighter at a retirement home? Seems unfair

hey im Lawrence
you're very pretty by the way
before you delete my message, i just wanted to tell you a little about me so you have an idea of who i am and show you im not like these other guys on this site
im nice, fun, outgoing, laid back, caring, and a gentleman
also real, honest, trustworthy and faithful
i go to school, I drive and own my own car
i am single, and not a liar, player, or a cheater
i would like to get to know you (:

hey love im kevin im just a simple man hard working love to hang out well idk if i wright more u wony hav much to ask so yea im the guy for u

"I wrote you 365 letters. I wrote you everyday for a year."

Since you enjoy "The Notebook" would it be okay to do this? lol.. kidding. I won't even write back if you don't respond the 1st time :D

Anyways, I had to search the internet for that quote (took atleast 40 seconds of googling) ... So hopefully you'll take 40 seconds and write back lol

Hope you have a great day!

-Andy

> *EDITOR'S NOTE:*
> BTW, this guy wrote back...3 times

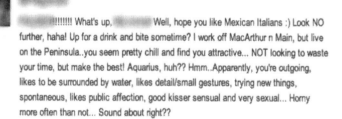

!!!!!!! What's up, ████ Well, hope you like Mexican Italians :) Look NO further, haha! Up for a drink and bite sometime? I work off MacArthur n Main, but live on the Peninsula..you seem pretty chill and find you attractive... NOT looking to waste your time, but make the best! Aquarius, huh?? Hmm..Apparently, you're outgoing, likes to be surrounded by water, likes detail/small gestures, trying new things, spontaneous, likes public affection, good kisser sensual and very sexual... Horny more often than not... Sound about right??

So, up for that drink sometime? :)

Milton

WTF?!

"The insane, on occasion, are not without their charms."

– Kurt Vonnegut

Hey! Can I talk to you about Jesus for a minute? Did you know...that I don't actually wanna try to talk to you about Jesus. That's not exactly what this site's for. Let me guess, every other message is just creepy dudes saying "You're hot!" and that's about it?

Whats good baby you single? ;) your a cutie i would want to fondle with :) Lets kick it baby :)

Hey there boobs... Are you on here for a date? What exactly are your intentions?

Ur so pretty, but I don't care for implants.(i dated a lot of strippers) if ur personality is kool, I would like to take u to a dodger game?

> EDITOR'S NOTE:
> I can relate. I don't care for fast food, but I'm always at McDoalds

You said your the life of the party and everyone calls me party marty so if we p artied i bet it would be fun haha im always out and if you like goin out youll have fun w me.. Im.pretty hooked up. haha Your also cute so that helps to and you seem pretty chill and down to earth based on what you said in your.profile. What you think?

sup girl ill tell you str8 i know u dont was to be reading but, i can take you out and make your fairy tales come 2 live

Hi great smile

I come to Cali often

Would you like to communicate and meet up when I'm down soon?

> EDITOR'S NOTE:
> (Robot voice) Let-us-co-mmun-i-cate

I would love to get to know you and hopefully take u out on a date with dinner and then possibly take some pictures of you by the beach so we can watch the sunset!!!

> EDITOR'S NOTE:
> ...and then you murder me

Marry me   ? :)
Fuck the bullshit! Lol jk!

Why you are so beautiful to my eyes, you can just make me go blind *.*

Don't ignore my message... Trust me lol What you up to hun ;)

Your pritty much are the bombest girl on this sight and ill tell u one think im not the same ol borning guy from ur highschool......im ricky btw im from the eastcoast connecticut to be exact. i hafta say u have no compition on this sight at all i mean if u like what u see or if anything appeals to u on my page i have more feel free to email me back id be more than glad to talk to u.. U probly have a million messages so im not gonna try and waist ur time hope to hear from ya

Hi! Do you know how much a polar bear weighs? Enough to break the ice Hi the names Joel! You seem down to earth and real, not to mention very beautiful!!! Not many girls have these qualities, it's like finding a diamond in the grass it just doesn't happen! I think we should jump and see where we fall!

> ### EDITOR'S NOTE:
> Diamonds in the grass? It's diamond in the rough dumbass

Your literally portrayed on here as the biggest slut. I'm a model myself, carry yourself some dignity. What has the world come to

Do you drink milk with ice?

Hola como estas!?! :) I just had to say Hello!!..you are extremely beautiful! I have a gut feeling you are just as beautiful on the inside but I wanted to see that for myself! ;) lol..you should definitely hit me back I would enjoy making you smile!

> ### EDITOR'S NOTE:
> Let me get this straight, you're going to check out my insides and make me smile? I'm in

Hey how's it going? I'm Reymundo, what's your name?
Have you ever gone on a date and played laser tag? Against a bunch of mean, ruthless, hyped up on mountain dew kids? Lol sounds fun

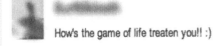

How's the game of life treaten you!! :)

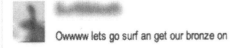

Owwww lets go surf an get our bronze on

:) aight soo like you said you get a bunch of messages and I hope MINES stands out. Its undetstandable tho. Your beautiful. I doubt that you'll reply:/ but if you happen to read this hope you keep doin what you do and enjoy life :) stay up

> EDITOR'S NOTE:
> For the record, this guys is not black

You are sooooo gorgeous! If you don't mind big dogs, they love taking pictures being kissed... ;)

Hey there gorgeous. Finally a beautiful girl with brain in her head. Shit. Anyways, who into any extreme sports?

> EDITOR'S NOTE:
> Yeah, good thing I have a brain. Shit. I be into extreme sports

Hi my name is EJ, and i would love to model with you. Im gonna be honest but i have pretty sexy undies ;) lol...

Knock.knock!

EDITOR'S NOTE:
No ones home

I was. My girlfriend passed away about a year ago, and for a whole year I wasn't talking to girls aha but now I feel like I'm ready

Idk why that sent to you! Mybad aha

EDITOR'S NOTE:
It sent because you wrote it and pressed send

Wassam with you

EDITOR'S NOTE:
Wassam!

6/18/20

If you want to have some fun from a Guy from Long Beach Message me back cause im sick of all the girls i know from high school lol what a coincidence!

The following images were attached to this message.

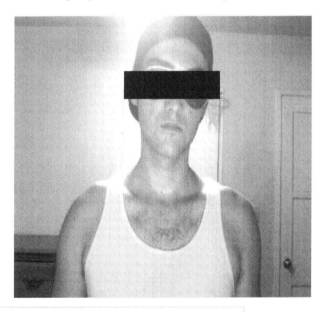

EDITOR'S NOTE:
Maybe when we hang out I can watch you commit a terror attack

Hey cutie we should chat it.. pretty sure we would have a blast of a time!! Im Matthew btw [redacted]! I didnt read Golf u ever play that? An fuckk Yeahh i was pulling for the clippers too this year.. o well They have a good shot Next.. James should win it... an u dont be lame an dont write backk LameO :p

> EDITOR'S NOTE:
> Gonna go ahead and be lame

Wow ur very beautiful...maybe I can introduce u to a couple of people if ur into doing pin up for cars bikes n tattoo shops. Well enough of the bizness side... Hit me up some time so we chat n hangout

Hey goodnight.

> EDITOR'S NOTE:
> He literally opened and closed in two words

has used some points and bought you this gift!!!.

CLIPPER FAN !! I got season tix !!!! Huge CP3 fan.. Anyway besides that I was honestly about to cancel this damn account.. I got like 4000000 messages and they are all from fat mexican girls..I feel so out of place here but then I bubped into your profile and ummmmm HI!!! !!! :) Where in Irvine are you?! :)

PS.. I didn't knwo the stupid bear sticker said I love you .. It was tiny I thought it was like NICE TO MEET YOU or something lol.. Don't judge !

> **EDITOR'S NOTE:**
> Yeah, a lot of red bears with roses say "nice to meet you"

Hey names Dave here... hanging out beach party are the only words I focused from your profile and I also love to hit beach
parties if you can talk and hang I have beach parties to hang at if up for it. but this is my ice/deal breaker.
what music are you into?

DH

Boating ... July seven in the keys ... Take your sexy Ass ...

heyy really hope u havetime to read my message becausr your so cool and stuff ;) lol im really funn i promisee hah

letsss go to the beachh vlbeachh

Well you know I got this blunt rolled up on the table and he wants your lips to smoke him ;)

I will, I am

EDITOR'S NOTE:
I won't

Hi

If you're the life of the party, and I'm the life of the party, do you think something catastrophic might happen if our worlds collided? Maybe it's better if we don't meet...BUT, maybe, just maybe we could burn like fabulous yellow roman candles exploding like spiders across the stars. And that might be really fun. Let me know if you're interested.

-J

Lol the miami heat the champions come in get that pussy ate out !

Estas muy linda corazon! you have such a courageous smile

EDITOR'S NOTE:

"In my country a women does not smile in public, you have much courage!"

You seem like a spunky vixen!

How about this for a first date? We'll go around the country robbing banks together! You be the stick up gal; I'll be the getaway driver guy! We'll wear Bonnie and Clyde masks for the job! We can even give half the money to charity!

It'll be totally epic! We'll get super rich and save the world at the same time!

ok do u like milk with ice cubes?

Shimmy Shimmy Yea

Hahaha... Don't be lame. Let's rip this Heli around then I'd you don't wanna be lame.... Do you get scared of sharks in the ocean? Just trying to see what my boundaries are...

Crazy stalker.looking.to take.sweet girl on Hollywood walks lol not a.stalker but artist painter.and am familar with.People chasing.there.dreams.cuz I only.hang out with People.that want the.best for them. Selfs when ever r u going to.read yr msgs by the way I'm from la but.my.heart is the world.and my.home. Is under the.sun and moon my likes are music entertainment and experiencing socially my 6 senses

> *EDITOR'S NOTE:*
>
> I think this guy had a seizure while he typed this

Hi I'm Michael would you like to go out on a date with me and maybe after go to best buy? :)

How about some stream of conscious?

Hi,

How are you doing?

I love the beach too. My favorite beach is at a resort area in Greece called Kassandra in Halkidiki. Have you ever been there?

Chris

> *EDITOR'S NOTE:*
> This is going to sound crazy, but I'm there right now

Hey First thing first I'm not tryin to get laid. I'm also not trying to get married .I'm just trying to meet someone cool as shit and from what i got from your profile you seem like a really cool chick .Your also very pretty which doesn't hurt so do you wanna be friends drink something dance party and get weird All night or we can go to Barnes an noble and get lost for hrs whatever lol

shut up... no one cares....

Persistence

"The most essential factor is persistence – the determination never to allow your energy or enthusiasm to be dampened by the discouragement that must inevitably come."

– James Whitcomb Riley

Anything and everything a respectful man would do to show a woman deserving how much he would love to be that hero in her life... You are the perfect example of why life is so worth living but also how much living is not fully lived

You get men fighting for your attention everyday dont you? See I dont play that game. Being with someone goes further than just looks. You are probly the most gorgeous young lady I ever lay my eyes on... But what kind person are you? You just date? You looking for a friend or a relationship?

Let me know if you care to ever kiss...

How do I find you? Ill leave right now to pick you up...

6/19/2012 6:41:50 PM

Holy shit what's up lol

6/20/2012 4:01:19 PM

holy shit i would motor boat the hell out of them tigo bitties lol

 6/19/2012 6:41:45 PM

Hello miss lady, hope I come of very creeper so I stand out from the rest of the messages. Just kidding! Well kinda. I read your description and thought you know what challenge accepted. So here I am messaging a cute girl hoping she will message back haha.
My name is Eric, what's yours??

6/19/2012 7:25:50 PM

If no interest in me I do know models and see if they can give you references to their agencies

6/19/2012 12:25:44 PM

heyyy :o)

6/20/2012 2:39:44 PM

screew all the lames and fuck games the real deal holy field

6/18/2012 4:20:43 PM

hi woman what are you up too?
im sammy

6/20/2012 12:24:06 AM

wanna go to vegas in a week for my birthday

6/18/2012 3:40:46 PM

Hey gorgeous

6/19/2012 6:31:38 PM

Hey gorgeous

6/18/2012 4:02:59 PM

Wow you are absolutely georgeous! Why is a beautiful girl like you on such a stupid web sight like this?

6/18/2012 6:01:51 PM

You are really the most beautiful girl I have ever seen in my life and defiantly on this sight my name is Michael.

6/19/2012 7:43:44 PM

Wow you are absolutely georgeous! Why is a beautiful girl like you on such a stupid web sight like this??

6/23/2012 12:48:34 AM

Hey beautiful

6/23/2012 12:50:36 AM

Looking for something real funnand everything. I want long term and hopefully marriage so if you want to chat hit me up

6/19/2012 6:38:45 PM

I met you at UCI. Do you remember? I am Tony

6/19/2012 7:35:47 PM

i believe you get a lot of messages. take a look at your pictures lol. we should model together :) i am Tony

> EDITOR'S NOTE:
> I am Tony. I am Tony

6/18/2012 3:57:03 PM

Hello █████ u seem amazing and down to earth. Hit me back if U want to chat sometime.. I would love to hear from u..

6/18/2012 4:12:52 PM

Hello █████ u seem amazing.. Hit me back if Ur down to chat sometime.. I would love to hear from u..

6/18/2012 4:41:13 PM

Hey you if your looking to be spoiled then hit me back..

6/18/2012 5:08:15 PM

You must get Tons of email on here.. Hit me back If Ur down to chat..

6/19/2012 6:16:53 PM

Hey █████ u seem like a great person to talk to.. Hit me back if u want to chat sometime. I would love to take u out and have fun. Let me know if ur down..

6/19/2012 6:55:52 PM

Hey u I guess u get tons of emails to respond back lol..

6/19/2012 7:23:42 PM

Damn Ur freaking a 10 lol

6/20/2012 3:38:15 PM

Hey beautiful how's life treating you? Whats new with you hottie?

6/18/2012 5:00:25 PM

Hi there :) I'm Danny

 6/18/2012 5:04:33 PM

I just moved out here from Salt lake I need to make some cute new friends like you! :)
hope to hear back from you. I know you get like 9 billion messages a day.

 6/19/2012 11:55:57 AM

Lemme know when you have some extra free time, I'd like to get to know you.

Hi my profile on here keeps freezing and its hard for me to send you messages so Im
going to delete this profile but I like the way you carry yourself and I want to get to
know you more so I can take you on a date so can I get your number?

hi its good to meet you :-) my name is Sean and I actually took time to read your
profile even though most people don't read profiles, I like what you said in your profile
and I just wanted to say sorry if I seem like I was rushing when I asked for your
number but my profile keeps freezing and its hard to send you this message but I
hope you get this message but I really am trying my best :-) to get to know you
because I like the way you carry yourself even though it might seem like im rushing
I'm not think about it there's plenty of men that take there time but there still bad guys
because most men are bad so please don't let me asking for your number overshadow
that I'm a nice guy so look I'm not trying to rush I'm just being honest and saying the
only way to get to know you is if I get your number since my profile is freezing, so can
I get your number?

Hi beautiful!! I am Ryan, a local bartender. May I ask you a couple questions?

Ps. You are 22, please don't message me if you live with your parents.

Hey!! :)

6/18/2012 8:10:19 PM

Hey :)

6/19/2012 12:14:34 PM

Hey I think your the most beautiful girl I've ever seen :) and I'd live to get to know you
:)

6/20/2012 4:03:50 PM

Hey sexy you real

6/21/2012 8:51:44 PM

Want to go jetsking

6/21/2012 8:52:19 PM

How are you tonight sexy

6/21/2012 8:55:00 PM

I want you

6/21/2012 8:56:21 PM

6/20/2012 3:53:02 PM

Hey ████ my names Jonathan so you seem like a pretty amazing chick, honest to that's rare so I thought I would see what you like to do on your fun time and maybe get to know each other a little

 6/20/2012 3:54:19 PM

Hey ████ my names Jonathan so you seem like a pretty amazing chick, honest to that's rare so I thought I would see what you like to do on your fun time and maybe get to know each other a little

 6/20/2012 3:54:22 PM

Hey ████ my names Jonathan so you seem like a pretty amazing chick, honest to that's rare so I thought I would see what you like to do on your fun time and maybe get to know each other a little

 6/20/2012 3:54:27 PM

Hey ████ my names Jonathan so you seem like a pretty amazing chick, honest to that's rare so I thought I would see what you like to do on your fun time and maybe get to know each other a little

 6/20/2012 3:54:30 PM

Hey ████ my names Jonathan so you seem like a pretty amazing chick, honest to that's rare so I thought I would see what you like to do on your fun time and maybe get to know each other a little

 6/20/2012 3:54:34 PM

Hey ████ my names Jonathan so you seem like a pretty amazing chick, honest to that's rare so I thought I would see what you like to do on your fun time and maybe get to know each other a little

 6/20/2012 3:54:38 PM

Hey ████ my names Jonathan so you seem like a pretty amazing chick, honest to that's rare so I thought I would see what you like to do on your fun time and maybe get to know each other a little

6/19/2012 3:19:13 AM

You is fine girl. I need some of that

6/20/2012 10:37:15 AM

Let's go around the city you model I take photos

has been deleted

6/25/2012 7:10:10 PM

I think you are so so sexy. I would love to chat and get to know you

has been deleted

6/26/2012 4:54:51 PM

Chat!

6/21/2012 4:25:12 PM

Well I thought about it for a second...do I want to be Mr. Funny haha and try to make you laugh right off the bat. Nah! That would make me seem to goofy. Do I want to be Mr. Rico Suave and try to woo you to death! Nah that would make me seem way too serious...since this whole online thing is decided within the first 4 lines of the convo! I think I'll go traditional and say...hi =)

6/25/2012 4:43:28 PM

So we're robbing a bank and we need a getaway to triumph our new found fortune! Where are we going?

hi i saw ur profile and pik cause i guess u looked at mines..lol i must say ur a very beautiful woman :) whats ur nationality if i may ask? by the way im michaelimcuban born there camewhen i was 5. im new to this actually been on here couple days little optimistic about this whole online dating cause there's alot of weird as people. but w.e. u never know if u dont try :)

hello hope ur doing good!! i read ur profile and i must say u seem interesting im very str8 up person so ima be me :) and ur so my style i like hehe well im looking for a friend i was in a long term relationship before recently single,but little by little getting an itch lol we can meet have drinks if we both click meaby have more fun after hehe . yes i know im too honest but i like to be that way this is not my thing normally but what can i say it happens lol little about me im latin nice shape like to work out got couple tats and im pretty down to earth i like to laugh and joke around well wanted to say something u never know if u dont try :) thx and up to u

EDITOR'S NOTE:

Seven minutes apart

Pathetic

"The most pathetic person in the world is someone who has sight, but no vision."

– Helen Keller

Hey ████████ I'm David nice profile definitely. Caught my eye I'm writing you this MSG idk why but I am lol not that I don't have any confidence in a reply back from you but I'm 100% positive that you are swarmed with a shit load of messages lol and it must hard to filter thru them and see who's fake and a douchbag ha hah but anyways I'm pretty Lagit just seeing what's out there if you like to know more me msg me back please do so lol

See idk y a guy like me has try so hard to get with our even to hang out with a girl like u... U r gorgeous n I would just like the chance to be able to hang out with u some time. ;)

Hey hows it going I'm Johnson I was reading your profile and thought what would stand out to you considering you probably get a ton of messages. I decided that I would just ramble on and make it long and useless to read because I bet no one has tried that approach lol. Anyway hope you write back lol ;-)

To be perfectly honest, I think your one of the prettiest girls I've seen in a long time but I'm pretty sure you get that alot on here lol. I would really like to get to knw you if your ok with that. Maybe you feel the same way idk. We may have alot in common. Im really a great guy to get to knw. If your not interested it's totally fine, but I sure hope I hear back from you!

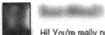

Hi! You're really pretty and you seem like an awesome girl. I'd love to take you out sometime to get to know you. Let me know if you're interested.

-Sean

Ps this is legit. I really want to get to know you. No bs. I know I'm probably one message from a normal guy in the mix of a bunch of creeps. Let me prove to you that I'm a gentleman. Hopefully I'll stand out..

What are you looking for in a guy? How do you feel about video games and technology in general?

Ok I know you've received 1000 message already, but this one is different... I bet I can make you laugh, I bet I can make you sing, just read my profile. So talk to me... :)

Hi. My name is Tristan. Im not sure what to say. Lol. Apparently I get nervous and my brain stops working when I try to speak with a pretty girl. If I havent totally failed here drop me a line. Id like to know the person behind those beautiful eyes. Take care.

EDITOR'S NOTE:

Love the confidence

I was quite surprised by how down-to-earth you seem in your profile. Hope you get a chance to check mine out. How many messages do you get in a day? How long have you been modeling?

Would you mind telling me why you declined please? I'm not tryin' to bug, but would really like a chance to get to know you a little better

hi im aiden....honestly idk wht to say to make u wana rite back...idk what kind of girl u are..i dont know anything but whats ritten on here...but im hoping ur a romantic sweet girl looking for more than sex or a hookup...looking for a guy with nothing but good intentions ....looking to hopefully find a cute girl worth being in a relationship with....i dont want just any girl just cuz i feel the need to be in a relationship...which i dont.....i wana be in a relationship so that i can have the girl who makes a difference in my life.....if der isnt a girl like that then i dont need a relationship to be happy....we live in miami....ppl have meaningles relationships all the time...what i want....is sumthing that matters....i hope i stood out...because u stood out to me...im not afraid to put myself out der...doesnt mean im weak...im strong..i just have respect for the dating world lol...and i dont play games...

EDITOR'S NOTE:

Der, der, I'm strong

Ummmm wow your are really really pretty. I would love to talk and get to know you and maybe get a drink or dinner? Lol this is my first time on one of these sites so I don't really know what to say, I hope I don't sound dumb. But I really hope to hear from you :)

hey whats up? nice pics...really nice pics lol.i bet you taste as good as you look lol i wouldnt be surprised if you never message me back bcuz youll probably never get to my message in your crammed inbox lol.. its all good hope to hear from you take care

> *EDITOR'S NOTE:*
>
> I actually got your message and no

So I think your very hot I also like what you say you seem cool and sweet I love it lol well I bet you never take a second look or write back I know your to fly for a guy like me lol well I just had to say "wow your a sweet tart" :)

oooo, pick me, pick me!
:))
seriously now,

I'm Raz, and I think you really are sweet and sexy and I think we would look great together. I would love to take you out and get to know you better.
If you like my proposal, hit me back.
:*

Hey there! Just thought I'd drop by and tell you that you have caught my attention and I just HAD to say hi ;) Well, hope I catch your eye! Maybe grab your attention as much, lol... Can't wait to get a chance to know you ;) ... And of course, have some great adventures together!! Haha...
oh and yea... Omg wow! you are BEAUTIFUL!

Hi there _____ this is Chris ,just wanted to say that your page caught my attention. I think youre absolutely gorgeous and stunning. I really like how you described yourself with your words. You seem like a great woman with great qualities.You just seem like a fun, outgoing woman with a great personality.

I would really love a chance to chat and get to know you. All I can say is that I'm a great guy with a good heart and good head on his shoulders. I really think I may have all the qualities you would want in a guy.I think we could really connect. I come at you with all respect and good intentions.Hope to get your attention

So tell me _____ what does a cool, fun, down to earth sweet guy need to do to get your attention. I'm writing to you again to express my interest and let you know i really want to get to know you. I'm sure you get a lot of messages from guys saying this and that but I'm sincere in all I'm saying. I seriously have a li_____ crush on you since I first saw your profile. I think you have such a beautiful smile. It really seems like we can connect well. I'm a very all fashioned guy with good morals as well. I can definitely make you laugh and smile. I'm a guy who has his life together, has his career established, just bought his house and in school to get my masters. Just want a chance to chat and get to know you. I really think we can relate, im looking to meet people that are at my level and have good things going for them. I come at you with all respect. Get to know me, you won't regret it.

_____ has been deleted

hi let's have fun :)

(I'm also very smart if you care about that sort of thing haha)

I'm also open to friendly chat, I promise I'm very interesting

hey i just saw your pictures....and this is crazy.....but you're a heavenly blessed beauty.....so respond to me maybe

Ok, I know you're absolutely swamped with messages right now, but hear me out. I promise this one is different, I'll prove it! I've got the perfect line, are you ready to be amazed??

"hey ur cute how r u"

has been deleted

I'm usually not the best with sending messages, haha. It's much easier in person, ya know?

I think we'd get along very well. But then again, that's up for you to decide lol.

I'm not too sure how to make this message different, or more interesting than the rest that you get sooooo here it goes. Whenever I stop by my parents house, my mom is always talking about how I'm her cute little "Social Butterfly" haha.

I'm Eric by the way.

has been deleted

Hello there =) I know this is really random, and by the look on your face i can tell you're about to block me..and yes, I can see through the monitor =). I just wanted to take the time to ask if you'd like to go out sometime?

If I saw you at the mall and gave you a wink, would you give me a smile back?

Cut & Paste

"Originality is the art of concealing your sources."

– Benjamin Franklin

you make a very cute nerd, i'm very jealous of the dog in the picture, looks like he died and went to heaven lol. My name is Oscar btw aka cooler than the other side of the
pillow lol

Well you're flooded with messages but I see no harm adding mine to the pile. Would you like to chat a bit or get
together and see if anything develops? Looks like we live pretty close so that's a plus. Also, this thing says
we're a match. And really, who are we to argue with the internet? When you think about it, it's almost stupid
if we don't hang out. ;)

-Nathan

How r u? I'm Tommy I truly enjoyed reading about you and are very interested in learning some more. I don't know what a
beautiful girl like you is doing on here. Here are a few things about me, I'm very mature and grounded for my age, and I love
the beach, to cuddle, mtn bike, cooking, and traveling. I am not much of a bar party person and would much rather stay
home cuddle up to a good movie and cook dinner. I have never been a big partier or drinker. I'm looking for something
serious. I don't date around and are very down to earth and simple. So enough about me tell me some more yourself. Hope to hear from u
soon
Tommy

lol read your profile... and yes i believe there are 2 sole mates for every individual ... sometime u have to loose one in order to find the other one....

you seem super funny....

like u love to laugh and have fun...

thats whats up... yolo.... hit me up... lets chat...i bet our personalities will make it one crazy as party...lol :P

I have to say, you're very attractive. I wish I cld tell u that I was here to find my princess and that I cld be your Prince

Charming. But unfortunately I'm not in a position to tell you that. What I can tell you is that I'm a very honest and

upfront person. I'm not on this site to meet new friends, I'm looking for someone I can spend some time with and

enjoy some good times together. I'm currently in a relationship that is on downwards spiral. I don't see this

relationship lasting and I'm looking for someone new who might be able to occupy my spare time and eventually

maybe my heart as well. Anyways, I can't promise u that this will lead to anything long term, but I can promise you that

you'll always now where we stand. I don't like having to lie to people, so I feel its easier to be blatantly honest, even if i

knw the truth will get me in trouble. Anyways, let me knw if you are interested in meeting me. If so, send me your

email address or phone number and I'll send you more pics. Hope to hear from you.

I know exactly how u feel. I get tired of going thru all the msgs that just say hi or hey sexy. As flattering as it can b it

doesnt stand out or really get my attention. But wat did get my attention r ur huge sexy beautiful eyes;) im greg btw we

should get to know eachother

Well I thought about it for a second...do I want to be Mr. Funny haha and try to make you laugh right off the bat. Nah! That would make me seem to goofy. Do I want to be Mr. Rico Suave and try to woo you to death! Nah that would make me seem way too serious...since this whole online thing is decided within the first 4 lines of the convo!

I think I'll go traditional and say...hi =)

Ugh I'm too busy to come up with a clever message but get back to me if you want and I'll think of something more orignal.
You're super cute. haha

EDITOR'S NOTE:

Writing you this message to let you know I'm too busy to write this message

Hi sweetheart you are very beautiful.
I know you hear this 5 times a day but,
Where's your man at?
I wanna know
if you have time
for a nice guy
in your life
and if so, when?
Hit me up with the answer k.
I hope you have a nice day.

After a rigorously brief overview of your profile, I wanted to let you know I have already married and divorced you in my mind.

Thanks for all the wonderful imaginary memories... you will always have a special place in my heart.

Your ex-hubby,
Conor

Hey _____ Hows it goin ? My namez ruben.! I stay in chino ca looking for new n exicting fun people to hang out with maby more
I really enjoy going to the beach haveing fun and experiencing new things. i like the clippers otherthen the lakers so thats a plus lol :) i also
love to goin to clubs here n then n drink .but not all the time i love to Watch movies go to the drive in and i no how to cook so i can cook up a
nice romacituc meal :p .. I think u r realy gorgeous and u seem like a fun and unique girl to hang out with and get to no a lil better. I no u say u
have alot of messages but i hope im one of the ones u rite bak lol.. Well i hope to here from u soon feelfree to rite me wnever u can :)

Hi , im boe i liked ur profile, lol i dont have much on, sry im new to this thing, it kind of seems cheesy.. how do
you like this site?? Wow i sound lame lol

I hope you're having a great week and getting ready for some weekend fun. I Love your profile and the
energy in your pics. I'd like to grab a drink or coffee with you sometime. What are you up to today?
What's your name and number?
-Dave

Hola ████ have to say that your profile caught my attention: im a fun, outgoing, sporty, flirty guy myself. I can definitely
say that we would connect/compliment each other well. Hope I catch your attention and you take interest in getting to know
me, i won't disappoint you...

well a quick snap shot about me.. im Cesar, mexican/puerto rican. I live in Santa Ana/Orange area. I love to dance, have a
good time, im outgoing, fun, funny, flirty, romantic, educated, independent... but also have a manly edge to me. I have two
piercings, 7 tattoos, dimples, etc...

let's chat soon, summer is here... new friends, good time, =)

Hit me up!!

The following images were attached to this message.

I kno most likely u've had messages from dudes sayin "U DTF?", etc. I'm not gonna come
up to u in that sort of manner. Has this site worked out for u at all?

Hey there! How are you? Just wanted to say hi and also I think you and I would get along great! Also tell ya a little about
me... I love the out doors and love to travel! Riding fourwheels is a big passion of mine most the time durring the
summer I'm at the beach riding. And I'm also a little bit of a country bot I have horses and love to ride them just as
much! Well check out my profile and let me know if you would like to chat. Hope to hear from ya

My friend came into the room while I was looking at your profile and told me that if I didn't message you, she would.

Now, she's straight, so that's probably an empty threat but she does have an eye for pretty chicks so I'm totally going
to trust my mom's judgment on this one.

Let me know if she's correct or else I swear to sweet baby Jesus I'm going to list her on eBay. It's up to you to be a
super heroine & save mom or else: Jello time for my mommy...& a side order of strained peas & carrots...haha 🐱

Hey !!!!
Pay attention !!
Great guy here looking to meet
Some real people for a friendly outing
What do you say ???

Creepers

"I love creepy old dudes. I love that they have so much self confidence, despite having no evidence whatsoever to back it up."

– Ke$ha

Hello [redacted] Would you like to model in body art?

U are so sexy!!! That things I would to do u!!!!:))))

Dam baby girl you got that good shit man lol I couldnt be celibate with you lol fuck no!

I'm sure you get the same old emails over and over again. The ones where you're told you're gorgeous and sexy and blah blah blah. Well all of that is true but I was wondering if you have the personality and smarts to back up those lovely physical features of yours. I actually really want to find out and see who you are. Maybe even become friends or more. Let me know if you are interested.

Brad

P.S. Can I just have you? Please? Not in a creepy I own you sort of way. But in a lets go on a date and get to know each other, explore, get lost and laugh all night sort of way. What do you think?

EDITOR'S NOTE:

Man, I bet you wish you could take back that P.S. section

Not gonna lie totally one im trying to see you, two im definitley trying to take you home!! Let me know ;)

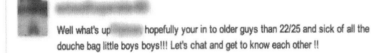

Well what's up _____ hopefully your in to older guys than 22/25 and sick of all the douche bag little boys boys!!! Let's chat and get to know each other !!

> **EDITOR'S NOTE:**
> How did you know I was into creepy old men?

I would love chat sometime about what you want or anything else you like..., i am 6-6" tall with blonde hair and blue eyes 9+ inches , feel free to contact me at blondemark31 at yahoo .I would definately love to see more of you, i do have pics i can send. Im not ugly, i know you will like;) just let me know what you want to see..;)hit me up, i am fun

> **EDITOR'S NOTE:**
> 9th eyes?!

Yah I bet soo with those pics I'm straight forward you have some great twins there lol but besides that your very pretty hi there

stogies

keggers

and manhattan.

quite a combo.

this means we should shoot some pool(8-ball) @ SoHO Billiards. (I suck, but it's fun, we can share my stick..)

enjoy my Hot apple!

The following images were attached to this message.

EDITOR'S NOTE:
Cool lean for an old, creepy guy

Boobs!!!!!!!

Hi there, how's it going? :-)

How do you feel about slightly older and much, much taller men?

I admire how much you enjoyed the Chick Hearn statue; I wonder what you did to Gretzky?

Best Wishes,

Nick

> *EDITOR'S NOTE:*
> Sounds great old, tall guy. I'd love to feel like I'm getting molested

Hi ▓▓▓▓.. All I can think about is your breasts. No wonder you're the life of the party. You get more attention than the koala bears at the zoo I'm sure. :)

Steve

> *EDITOR'S NOTE:*
> Thanks for signing off with your name, creep

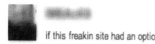

if this freakin site had an option to grade the fotos i would give 10+ to all your pics girl. i know you probably get 1000 messeges saying how hot and sexy you so i wont reapet it again instead please give me a chance so i can show it to you. i promise you wont be disappointed

First I must say you have beautiful eyes and a contagious smile. You seem fun. Do you date old men like myself? haha.

Hey _____, once I saw your profile I immediately knew what our first date would entail. If you're down :p

Love your either we click or we dont comment... That being said, hope to ttyl if you're attracted to older men..

Hey :) if u want more pics lemme kno

I will send u pics and videos for days :) nd you will like

 6/18/2

HI SEX

The following images were attached to this message.

6/17/2012 7:43 PM

EDITOR'S NOTE:

Hi, last person I'll see before I die

 !! I can please you with my tongue like no man!! You need to text me lol

Hows it going gorgeous? I wana make u scream my name! I also want to treat you with the respect you deserve and have an honest, good time. I can easily see why u get so many messages. I think we could have alot of fun. Message me if ur interested

First I wanna give u a dozen roses and then tell you are beautiful. Then take you too a wonderful restaurant then have a walk on the beach and sit and talk about each other. Your beautiful and have an amazing smile. I'm a Capricorn so we are going to click instantly and look at me I'm sexy ass fuck!!!!!!!

I wanna smell your feet

Damn girl....I would love for you to stick your pussy in my face and tell me to eat it. Would even stick my tongue deep in your pussy until u cum so hard!!!

Damn you are fine!

I would love to motorboat those tits and let you ride my hard cock

I think you'd be perfect for some bondage

Need your opinion! I have a poem here that I would like for you to read... Feel free to let me know if its extra cheesy alrite?

I think i've really fallen...

For a girl with so much passion.

A glimpse from her is considered deadly...

Yes a fatal attraction.

I never found the right words to say,

To her i remain nameless.

In an instance I lose touch of all reality in her presents.

I guess that labels me senseless.

I am engulfed into an intense fantasy,

The results of my burning desire.

Unbelievable love makin' that heats up as our hearts are racin'

Its her in first place and I follow as her secret admire

Wow. You've won the prize for THE GREATEST written profile.

I'm think I'm going to print this out and put it on my fridge... FOREVER!

Keep up the good work, you adorable lil nerd! :)

Boomer sooner??

Hey you, i'm just going to throw this out there. I find you very attractive and I would love to set up a FWB situation. I always make
the girl get off and I please in all the ways you would like to be pleased. Very discrete here. Let me know if you are interested in
something like this.

How's it goin? I have to ask if those are real

EDITOR'S NOTE:
You didn't HAVE to

Wow I would eat u all up

your hot (; u should sit on my face and ride my tounge (;

hey how r u?

The following images were attached to this message.

EDITOR'S NOTE:
Scared

Hey old man like you alot

i'd love you to cuff me and make me lick your body all night.

so I am a high school teacher looking for a young hot coed for some summer fun... and Im having no luck.. :(

You should have my babies

Wow your beautiful. Hows it going

If I woke up to you ever morning I would want your legs wrapped around my head

Guys Obsessed With Guys

"I know that you believe you understand what you think I said, but I'm not sure you realize what you heard is not what I meant."

– Robert McCloskey

Hey ████, maybe u should stop going for white boys latinos are way more fun

Good luck sorting through that morass my dear! The west coast, jeresy shore, douchebag types in LA clearly outnumber the gentlemen like 100 - 1, at least on the club/dating scene. Or perhaps their cologne overdoses and hyper conspicuous, one liner, DTF bullsh*t just karmically keeps the good dudes from even trying. It's a fake tanned, steroided, open shirted, one dimensional wonderland of 30 year old children with Ferraris and Amex Black Cards with more hair gel and trust fund money than substance, depth, character and couth. Hell, they don't even know what couth means.

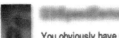

You obviously have not met a man yet. Message me when you are ready to meet one.

> EDITOR'S NOTE:
> For the record, this guy was 5'3" and 108 lbs ...a real man

Is it gay that the notebook is my favorite movie too? Hahha it's so well written! Plus Noah is a beast haha. Hi, I'm Anthony.

Hall of Fame

"No one's ever asked me to be in the Hall of Fame before. This is a first, so I'm going all the way with it. I'm going to take my shirt off, too."

– Bill Murray

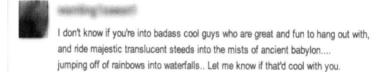

I don't know if you're into badass cool guys who are great and fun to hang out with, and ride majestic translucent steeds into the mists of ancient babylon.... jumping off of rainbows into waterfalls.. Let me know if that'd cool with you.

ill pay to eat u out

Hey ██████ I'm Nick...I work at CBS...do you always wear those glasses? :)

Hey I'm Nick...can you call or text me? I'm producing a Tv show that involves a yacht I wanna know if you wanna be a part of it.

EDITOR'S NOTE:
I don't know. This guy from ABC has
a show that involves a blimp...

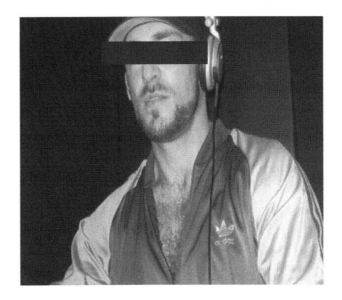

u sexy ass mutha fucka! whats up! fuk ur damn sexy i wanna wear legs as ear muffs so i can eat ur pie when i get hungry hahaha

I bet u squirt alot dont ya? ;p

The following images were attached to this message.

6/18/2012 4:19:51 PM

Let me know if you care to ever kiss...

6/18/2012 4:26:06 PM

How do I find you? Ill leave right now to pick you up...

6/19/2012 12:37:13 PM

You busy this weekend?

6/19/2012 3:10:27 PM

If I dont ask then the answer is always "no" right? How about we simply just hang out once see if its worth anything

6/20/2012 3:32:09 PM

You to good for a guy like me?

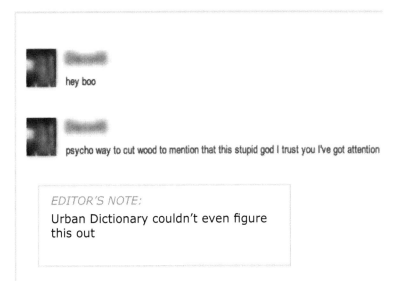

hey boo

psycho way to cut wood to mention that this stupid god I trust you I've got attention

EDITOR'S NOTE:

Urban Dictionary couldn't even figure this out

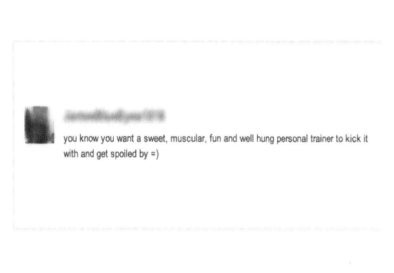

you know you want a sweet, muscular, fun and well hung personal trainer to kick it with and get spoiled by =)

Peggy Adams

Hey was just about to put away the old tackle box when I saw you swim by and was mesmerized by your fins.. Just throwing one last cast your way hope ya get snagged on my line !

How about a nice ride on my chopper to Disney and park hop all day, cool off at the water park, have a nice meal relax and talk in a hammock as the sunsets while we eat really good dark chocolate....

Hey doll...let's go to Vegas this weekend. I'm serious.

And if we went to Vegas...what would I do? What wouldn't I do? I would eat your pussy until you cum all over my face...then bend you over and watch your tits bounce as I fucked you from behind. Hard. Really hard.

Congratulations, you came up in my matches!!!!!!! I know right, you've been waiting for it! You can call everyone, let them
know. Tell your friends about it. You'll have to girl talk for at least five hours tomorrow about it. I mean, what are the
chances!

Ok, so I like to laugh and make everything into a sarcastic joke. It happens, right?

Now. I could write a resume. Tell you all about me. Like I am applying for the position of the guy you are going to hang out
with on Friday, or whatever. But that would be boring and dull. I might fall asleep doing that.

Wait, I could list out interrogation questions! Ask you things like what you do for fun? or maybe something really deep...
something like, "So where are you from?" You'd swoon, realizing that I care about where you are from and thus 'where
you're coming from'. You'd get "all a flush" at my wit, right?

Oh, I know, I could just delete all of this and type "Hey wazzup? Saw your profile. Ur cute! hit me back and we can
chat" That would probably work best. I mean, that's what everyone does right? So it MUST work! Shouldn't it?

How about instead, I do this. I am intrigued by your profile, and think it could be worthwhile to find out more about you.
You know, talk, and answer those age old questions, like:

"Is she a total basket case in hiding?"
"Will I fall asleep sitting next to her when we hang out?"
and don't forget...
"Is she just a guy with fake pictures, pretending to be a girl?!?!?"

So lets interact! Sound good? Glad to hear it! Lets get creative...

WE'RE GOING ON A ROADTRIP!!!!
So where are we going and why?

EDITOR'S NOTE:
Wow

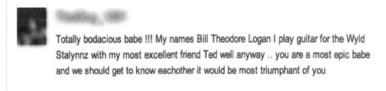

Totally bodacious babe !!! My names Bill Theodore Logan I play guitar for the Wyld Stalynnz with my most excellent friend Ted well anyway .. you are a most epic babe and we should get to know eachother it would be most triumphant of you

Guys Have No Game

I'm 8 in long 3 fingers wide, I love any position that make the women feel the best! But I like to deep stroke u while ur on ur back n ur legs ovr my shoulders, I will wear one if u want but if u don't want me to thn I won't, yes I will go down on u, and yes I have a pic of me shirtless and hard but I also have a closer pic of my hard cock!!

I'd start by kissing you and grabbing ur ass then I'd start to bite your neck as I rubbing you then I'd take off your clothes and pin you up against the wall with your hands above your head while I bite your neck and rub you all over then start to suck on your breasts and finger you then push you onto the bed and bite the inside your thighs whole rubbing your clit then start to suck on your clot and finger you then lick your lips and penetrate you wit my tongue and go in a circular

motion (; then id put it in slowly and get faster and faster then put your legs over my shoulders and deep stroke you hard and deep (; thn roll over and have you get on top and ride me while I thrust up into you! Then have you suck and choke on my hard hot cock then I would bend you over and fuck you harder and faster while I pull you towards me as I ram you from behind and make your legs shake then I would put your legs over my shoulders again and pound you as deep and hard as possible and make you scream from pleasure!!

Do you work? I am looking for a lady to support me while I lounge at home and drink, play video games, and scratch myself.

PS- Being able to cook is a plus...I am a huge bacon fan!

Stay tuned for volume 2

guyshavenogame.com

Koh Phangan, Thailand, Full Moon Party 2012 (seemed appropriate)

Left to right: Ian Gulbransen & Geoff Keith

About The Authors

Geoff & Ian are lifelong friends. Geoff Keith is a nationally touring headlining comedian born and raised in Southern California. As well as being a cast member on the hidden camera prank show MTV's "Disaster Date" for multiple seasons, he has also been featured on "Chelsea Lately," various VH1 Countdown shows, HBO, Comedy Central, BET, and the Late Late Show with Craig Ferguson. Keith resides in Burbank, CA where he performs regularly at all the local comedy clubs when he is in town.

Ian Gulbransen is an entrepreneur, traveler, and artist who maintains his day job as a Marketing Manager for a Silicon Valley startup. Gulbransen is a Seattle native who now calls Orange County, CA home.

Made in the USA
San Bernardino, CA
22 November 2017